A Scrabbled Mind

Zoe Pennant

Zoe Pennant

Author contact: zoejoseph3@yahoo.co.uk

Cover design by The Yellow Print Shop

Copyright Year: December 2016

ISBN: 978-1-909389-16-8

A Scrabbled Mind

Zoe Pennant

Dedications

I dedicate this book to all people that learn differently and think outside the box, we are truly gifted and have a learning style that others are still trying to figure out, how gifted is that?

Acknowledgement

Thank you

I would like to thank the Universe for allowing me an experience of a lifetime here on Earth.

Contents

About The Author: Zoe Pennant

I thought to myself I did not want to write as a third person to introduce myself, so here I am speaking to you as I write. I have a great passion to share and at the same time figure out myself, which has been a journey in itself, therefore writing a novel was a great way to share, be as creative as I wanted to be and still continue to experience more of who I was. *SO WHO AM I?* I am a being who is finding my way back home and until then I will continue to make a difference in the world by sharing experiences, one of the ways I do this is by writing and art. When you have read this novel you will somehow connect with the characters in some way or know someone that has and if that is the case, pass this book on when you have finished, it might just help that person in some way. By sharing this novel if one person gets something from it, then that will be great.

You are reading this book for a reason, now let us see what that reason is after you have finished it. Enjoy.

Zoe xxx

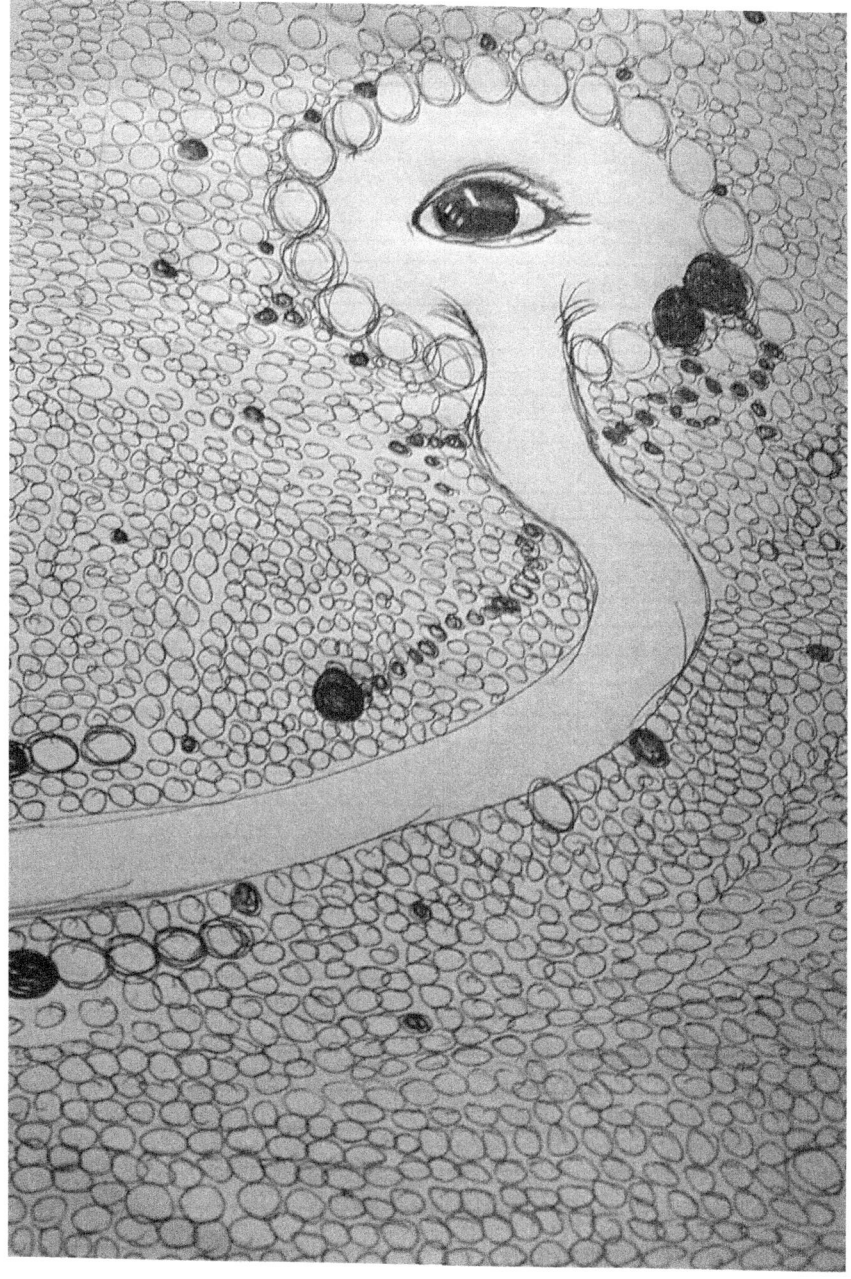

Prologue

They walked into the temple of consciousness, a place where there was no sound, time or space. A dark pureness surrounded this temple and waves flowed with a calmness that made love so tender where there was no need to touch, as it all was in the existence of nothingness.

"Why am I here?" It asked.

It replied, "You're about to embark on a beautiful journey of communication, understanding, feelings, fear, love, happiness, joy, selfishness, anger and the most important to you – patience."

It started to smile with excitement; the moment of waiting for this experience was now arriving and it felt the warmness of what it was hearing, even though there was no sound but just knowingness.

"What will I learn or do?" It asked.

"Well that depends on what you remember, you'll become a human force, now is the time to feel your own contract of what you choose to experience while on your journey, this is why you're here. I must state your journey will only last for eighty-two years, so please be wise about what you choose to experience.

"How do I know what to choose?" It said.

"We're here in the temple of pure love and togetherness," it replied, "it'll unravel itself to you......just embrace it."

A bright colour lit up the temple, where the conscious could hear, see and speak for the moment.

"Right my dear let's do this," it said.

It created its journey with the bright colour as its guide, everything it ever wanted to feel, see, hear, love, share, understand and fear got created within a moment. The bright colour suddenly disappeared allowing the pureness of the dark to re-appear.

"Are you ready?" It said.

"I think so, what happens now?"

"You'll wait for a sign to enter into your adventure. Please remember your journey is not real even though you'll feel like it is. Every thought, feeling, touch, taste and fear will only be an illusion of your journey that you've chosen, this is only a contract that you've experienced for yourself. When you start your journey a cord will be cut, all memory of this moment will be lost for you to re discover. Now you go off and enjoy it."

Chapter 1

London, 29th December 1974

"Push! Come on, you can do it! Push as hard as you can!" The midwife said. The midwife was encouraging Mrs Benjamin by holding her hand, while she placed a sick bowl by her side just incase she would start to vomit, Mrs Benjamin was starting to feel sick with all the pushing she was doing, her energy was becoming low where her sight of focus and concentration was starting to fade,

Mrs Benjamin was in great pain, a pain that cannot be described unless you could imagine a volcano bursting out of the earth, if there is such an imagination. This was her first time having a baby and nobody could have prepared her for the agony she was going through as she dripped with sweat, and drained from the pressure of screaming and pushing.

"That's it one more big push," said the midwife.

Mrs Benjamin gave a loud scream and the biggest push ever but the baby still refused to come.

"I can't take this any longer," she wailed and with some urgency, the midwife examined her. She frowned. The baby was becoming distressed.

"I'm going to have to use forceps to help the baby a little," she said calmly; in her experience a soothing voice helped temper any agitated patient.

"Why? What's happening to my baby?" Mrs Benjamin voice trembled.

"Your baby is becoming distressed so, we'll have to help it a little," the midwife smiled reassuringly as she explained about the forked equipment she held in a gloved hand. "It's better and safer if we use this, Mrs Benjamin. Is that ok?"

She hesitated. New to the use of forceps, she wasn't keen on using them but afraid for her baby's health she didn't hesitate to say yes.

The midwife manoeuvred the metal grip into place and gently stroking Mrs Benjamin's arm whispered to her to make one final and big push. Mrs Benjamin inhaled deeply, sucking in the air as if it was her last and with one massive blowout, gave one long huge push...a beautiful baby girl was born, awakening with loud crying.

The midwife beamed as she delicately held the baby for Mrs Benjamin to see her. "She's so gorgeous Mrs Benjamin," she said, wrapping her in a towel, "I'm just going to cut the umbilical cord and then she'll be all yours."

"Can we wait for my husband to arrive?" mumbled Mrs Benjamin but she knew he wouldn't be since he was out of the country. A lorry driver, he would work away for months at a time and even before being in the hospital Mrs Benjamin was extremely embarrassed that she would be giving birth alone. It was an experience she'd hoped wouldn't come to pass. But, it had.

"Sorry Mrs Benjamin, but we can't wait for long. Is he on his way?" The midwife asked.

Mrs Benjamin sighed and bowed her head. "It's ok, go ahead and cut the cord."

The midwife severed the umbilical cord before placing the baby in Mrs Benjamin arms; as soon as she does and with her eyes closed, the baby cried. It lasted for a joyous moment before she opened her eyes and stared at her mother.

It was difficult for Mrs Benjamin as the big innocent eyes looked into hers. Her heart beat as rapidly as it could and it wasn't long before she began to cry. She wept with joy. It had taken many years for Mrs Benjamin to become pregnant, at times she even thought it would never happen

"Do you know what you'll be calling her Mrs Benjamin?" asked the midwife.

"Oh yes, I've always knew if I had a girl I'd call her Ismay Violet Benjamin." The name was significant for Mrs Benjamin; she had dreamt it when she was 10 years old. It was a name she could never forget.

Chapter 2

June 1979. A summer's day. The sun was shining its long awaited beam on people who were excited to see it return after a couple of years since for the past two, it seemed the winter season was all year round. Loud music could be heard playing in people's homes and children romped in the streets, even the flowers seemed to suddenly blossom overnight. They looked fresh and colourful. On a few street corners, parents chatted with each other while the children laughed and messed around.

Life was beautiful, even if only for that moment.

Ismay was playing at the bottom of the stairs, her favourite place and not only did she enjoy playing on her own, she also loved having her imaginative and invisible friends as part of her tea parties while drawing colourful pictures; her best made up game.

She ran up the stairs, shouting, "Mum!"

Mrs Benjamin was making lunch. "Yes, my dear, how can I help you?"

"Why do I have to call you Mum but other people call you by your name?"

Mrs Benjamin laughed, stunned by such a question coming from a 5-year-old. "Mm, let me see," she replied, "children call their parents Mummy and Daddy because we give birth to you. Then, we give you a name for others to call you by. So you call me Mum since I gave birth to you while others call me by my name."

"But I still don't get it," Ismay persisted; a frown on her little forehead, big eyes squinting.

Mrs Benjamin always found it difficult to explain things to people much less her own daughter especially with her unusual questions. "Don't worry my child when you get older you'll understand. Let's get ready to go out into the lovely sun, we might as well make the most of it. Oh, your father will be home tonight." She added. Mr Benjamin was arriving home after four months working away.

They arrived at the adventure playground. Ismay loved it there since there was so much to do like playing on the slides, swings and going up and down on the seesaw. In a nearby hut, children could do painting, drawings and make things. The staff were friendly too.

At the rear of the adventure ground, Ismay went to pick flowers. She never played with the other children on the swings or slides. Mrs

Benjamin found a bench and sat, and soon another neighbour came to sit beside her. They started talking and a little while later, after the neighbour had left, she went in search of Ismay.

"Ismay what are you doing now?" She asked.

"I'm just picking some flowers for Daddy," came Ismay's reply.

Her mother could never understand the things she'd do. It seemed like her actions were that of a much older person rather than just a child. It was as if within her there was an old soul since she always had her own mind and would do things out of the ordinary, like either playing by herself or finding other children playing alone to play with. Even after her best efforts to get Ismay to integrate with other children, but this was what she loved about her daughter. Ismay was nothing like her or her Father and Mrs Benjamin thought maybe it was because she was an only child.

That evening Ismay's father - Mr Benjamin - arrived home. She loved spending time with her father and the first thing she did on seeing him was rush towards him, seeking to give him the flowers she'd picked earlier. Jumping into his open arms, he spun her round. She giggled. Smiling, Mrs Benjamin stared from across the kitchen.

Ismay had been so excited that she'd dropped the flowers and walking over, she picked them up before handing them to her husband. Reaching over, she hugged him and Ismay.

"Ok, ok Ismay let your Father breathe a little, he's here for the whole weekend this time, you know," she laughed, "and now there's dinner to do." She headed back into the kitchen to finish dinner while Mr Benjamin sat with Ismay on his lap. He began to tell her a story. Ismay loved listening to his stories. After dinner and with the evening slowly coming, it was time for Ismay to go to bed.

"Daddy, can you please read me a story?"

"Reading a story, right now my beautiful daughter, will take too long." Ismay looked saddened by his news. "But I can tell you another of my wonderful stories?"

"Ok!" Ismay joyously said. Her father started again, acting out the story by making funny faces, jumping up and down and acting out animal figures; leaving his daughter to laugh in delight. Eventually, with her falling asleep on his chest, he took her to bed and tucked her in. Giving her a hug, he whispered, "Good night, sweet dreams my love".

"Good night, Daddy," replied Ismay, sleepily.

Chapter 3

1989 wasn't a great time for Ismay and over the past ten years, so many changes had occurred. Her mother and father were now separated and she was struggling at school. Since she could be very self-opinionated and a plain talker, she wasn't getting on with her teachers. If Ismay felt something wasn't right or she misunderstood, everyone would know about it and the older she became, the more she realised people wanted her to be quiet, just shut up and do what she was told. Which she found naturally, very difficult to do.

"Ismay?"

"Yes Ms Healey?"

"Why can't I see your homework on my desk?"

"It's on your desk Miss, can't you see it?" Ismay responded, chuckling. She loved joking around with her teacher but Ms Healey was far from being amused.

"Stop messing around Ismay, you know you didn't put your work on my desk," stated Ms Healey, shaking her head. She was in despair. None of the other young people in her class ever tried messing with her like Ismay and sighing heavily, she watched Ismay.

She loved being a teacher, made time for students, however when they started to mess around, she had no time to waste; letting them know she was one person not to be messed around with.

The school bell rang. It was break time. "Everybody can go except for Ismay," addressed Ms Healey while the pupils hurried about, stuffing books into their bags and rucksacks.

Ms Healey wasn't smiling and she pondered what was wrong with Ismay. She was such a brilliant student but her pranks, uncaring attitude and outlandish behaviour were trying, even for her, a teacher of many years. She hated reading and she could never figure out why. One time, she'd asked Ismay to read aloud a section from a novel. Ismay had got up and began to read in a Scottish accent, causing the entire class to laugh and be disrupted. She'd even acted out the scenario, having her, Ms Healey, in stitches. To regain control and quieten the rowdy class, Ms Healey had shouted: "Ok class that's enough, Ismay if you can't do something without being silly then just don't do it. Please sit down and give someone else a chance. Thank you."

As busy as she was with the pressures of being a teacher, she always made time for Ismay, willing to support and help her as much as she could and seated behind her paper-filled table, Ms Healey asked, "What's going on with you Ismay? You're a distraction in class and are forever daydreaming. You're also behind with five pieces of coursework. Furthermore, the only subject you seemed interested in and on schedule with is Art. You do know this is your final year in school, right? Do you want to leave with no qualifications?" She sighed, shaking her head. "I really don't know what more to do with you. I've no choice but to get your Mother in to see Mr Akin."

Ismay shrugged her shoulders. "Blah, blah, blah! Do whatever you like Miss. Get my Mum in like I care, she'll probably be too busy anyway."

"This is exactly what I mean Ismay, your no-care attitude." She sighed again. "What's happened to you?"

Ismay said nothing and bowed her head to look at the floor. There was a moment of silence as Ms Healey shuffled some papers on her desk. Nothing was said, Ismay's eyes glued downwards, her hands behind her back; even to herself, she was unsure why she was acting the way she was and she knew Ms Healey wasn't the first person who was unable to get through to her. Ismay shrugged her shoulders again and still said nothing. As far as she was concerned nobody understood or cared and she, in turn, couldn't trust anybody with her feelings.

It was a week later when Ismay and Mrs Benjamin entered the Head Teacher, Mr Akin's office. The office was massive with everything in place. On his desk were framed photos of his family and a side cabinet with cups, sugar, milk, tea and coffee. Mr Akin was tall and slim and wore glasses. He was dressed better than most headteachers; designer shoes, trousers and semi-casual jacket, and like his clothes and office, he loved order around the entire school. For every student in the school, none wished to be taken to his office if they could help it.

A first generation African, who'd migrated from Nigeria a number of years before, his upbringing ensured he had particular values, such as respecting his elders and each other while still having his own voice. He was also encouraged to be confident and like other young

Nigerian children, was reassured by his elders to speak up for what he believed in.

"Please take a seat Mrs Benjamin and Ismay," Mr Akin said, gesturing to two vacant seats as he walked and sat behind his large table. It was bigger than Ms Healey's. He locked his fingers under his chin and they held up his head. He sighed, "Now where do I start? Can you please explain to me Ismay why you're not completing any work in class or at home?"

Ismay shrugged and stared defiantly at the head teacher. "I find it very boring. It doesn't stimulate me. Actually, I hate school and wish I didn't have to be here."

Mr Akin's sharp eyes never dimmed while he nodded. "So I see. Do you wish to leave school with no qualifications? What would your life be? How do you think you'd get a job?"

"No, I may not have any," Ismay replied, repeating her shoulder move. "I'm going to have my own business and work for myself."

Mr Akin nodded and said nothing for a while. "Don't you think this takes dedication, leadership, patience and an ability to never, ever give up? Plus, you'd need some kind of business qualification, do you think you have the quality to own your business based on how you are here at school?"

"Not at the moment," Ismay said, smirking as if she knew the answers, "but I'll have."

Mr Akin hummed in agreement and wrote on a slip of paper. "Ok, let's get back to your studying. You're in your last year and behind with your work, do you want to catch up or stay being bored and disrupting the class?"

Shrugging her shoulders again, Ismay grinned a little. "I don't think you're hearing me, I'm finding school and the subjects boring and really don't want to be here."

Mr Akin stared hard at both Mrs Benjamin and Ismay, thinking of a time when he'd dealt with a student called David in a previous school. There he was Head of Year and David had been extremely rude to his teachers. He just didn't care and with his anger and bad language, he'd act out by spewing the most unbelievable and nasty words while throwing things at his teachers. David's attitude was completely unbelievable but Mr Akin knew there was more to the boy than how he was behaving and when most teachers had given up on him, he hadn't. He couldn't put his finger on why David was the way he was, so, he gave David an ultimatum.

"It's up to you David. Would you rather stay here in school and have some counselling or be out? It's very simple."

Mr Akin never mixed his words and was always straight to the point. David listened and chose to have the counselling available within school. After a while the sessions resulted in him being a better person and after passing his exams and leaving the school, David ended up working in computers for a major international company. Mr Akin fully supported counselling, always having it as an option since his experience had shown him that some children had internal and external issues away from school and this had an impact on the way they behaved in school. However, with all the cuts schools were facing, he was unable to offer counselling to Ismay.

Mrs Benjamin coughed politely in her hand, interrupting. "Ismay, enough of your rudeness and have some respect for Mr Akin. He's the Headteacher of *your* school," Ismay stared at the floor but said nothing, "you, young lady, are grounded for a month until you have some respect for your elders and are up to date with your work. So that means no watching T.V. or going out - anywhere."

Ismay opened her mouth as if to say something but didn't.

"No Ismay, I really don't want to hear it. You're getting older and very soon will be leaving this school. You'd better change your attitude because the world out there isn't what you think it is!"

Mr Akin interceded, "Ok Mrs Benjamin, let's calm down." For a few moments, there was some silence in his office. "Would you like something to drink? Mrs Benjamin? Ismay? Tea? Coffee?"

Both Mrs Benjamin and Ismay shook their heads.

"Ok Ismay, are you fine with what your mum just said?"

Fidgeting with her fingers, Ismay shrugged. "Well it looks like I don't have much of a choice."

Mr Akin nodded, writing some more. "Ok, this is what we we're going to do. We'll put sufficient support in place and find a place for you to attend the various after school clubs. You have my word that you'll get the support you need."

Ismay looked up angrily and complained. "I don't need any help. I can do it by myself."

"So why aren't you?" Mrs Benjamin asked quietly, staring at her daughter. Ismay makes no reply.

"That's it then, right?" Mr Akin asked. Mrs Benjamin nodded while looking compassionately at her daughter. She looks so vulnerable, she thought. Now, as when she'd been born, there was an innocent and naïve look and she wished their current situation was different between them. There were challenges and as much as she was angry with Ismay, she wanted her daughter to achieve so much; more than what she'd ever achieved in her own life.

Mr Akin stood and walked to the door, followed by Mrs Benjamin and Ismay. He offered his hand. "Thank you for your time Mrs Benjamin."

Mrs Benjamin took it, shaking warmly. "Thank you for the meeting Mr Akin. I hope the school can give Ismay more support."

Ismay shyly avoided his eyes. Shaking Mr Akin's hand, she quickly left his office, hastily catching up to her mother. As they strolled along the corridor, Mrs Benjamin thought, if Ismay took on board what had just been agreed, there was a chance of her catching up, even at this late stage of her education. I wish she'd just focus.

But it wasn't to be…

The previous five years of school were the longest years of Ismay's life and being in an environment that misunderstood her, she was unable to connect or focus on her academic work and even on herself. She never understood why this was the case, even when she'd tried to apply herself as hard as she could. Finally, she left school without any qualifications. Even failing to pass her favourite subject - Art.

Chapter 4

Mr Benjamin grew up in a household where one was seen and not heard. Children weren't allowed to answer or suggest anything to their elders since they (the elders) were always right and children needed to always listen, first. His father was a functioning alcoholic and he was always drunk, most of the time. Every single day once he'd finished work and returned home, he'd drink himself to sleep. Because of his father's love for the drink, it caused him to never have a great relationship with his father. His mother, on the other hand, was always there to care and look after the children. She'd cook, clean and also worked part-time as a cleaner and as Mr Benjamin grew into a young adult, he witnessed the strained relationship between his parents, and many of their arguments would take place most evenings and around the children, this meant very little time or help whenever he did his homework. As far as he could see, his parents relied on his school to do it; including raising him and his siblings. At home, Mr Benjamin never saw his parents read books or newspapers, furthermore they never even read to him so he, in turn, found it very boring. He also recognised that both his parents found it hard to show any emotion, especially love, even though they still provided for the family and the children didn't want for anything. However, as he grew up, he struggled to show love to anyone, being uncomfortable with showing any emotion and finding it difficult to relate how he would truly feel.

He was good at his job and worked hard as a lorry driver, the only job he felt he was good at. Especially, since he couldn't read or write and was unable to understand words on paper, sometimes mixing up his words whenever he tried to write. Still, no one ever knew his challenges not even his wife and his driving job was the only place where he felt free as there was no reading or writing involved.

Then, Ismay came and grew up in his life at a time when his marriage was on the verge of breaking down and as his one and only child, he always made sure he was home from work, spending quality time with her. His love for her was unconditional but life had taken a major turn when his marriage with his now ex-wife, Mrs Benjamin, ended and since Ismay lived with her, he couldn't see her as regular as when they'd lived together. He missed her deeply but knew nothing of the impact his leaving the home had on her. A kind of map, in a way they all didn't expect.

For Mrs Benjamin, the breakdown of her marriage meant looking after herself and providing for Ismay - alone. Even though Mr Benjamin provided as much as he could, it never seemed to be enough. Her upbringing was very similar to her husband's, it was the one thing they had in common and in the early days, used to laugh so much about. But as time passed, they began to find it more and more difficult to communicate with each other and talk about the common things. Eventually everything became less and less, even their talks.

Sometimes, Mr Benjamin would get annoyed with his wife as he was unable to understand how disorganised she was. Once, when he bought their first car and they'd decided, as a family, to visit some cousins in Birmingham, he'd handed her a list of *written* directions rather than a map. He knew reading a map wasn't the easiest of things to do and to him, this seemed better and easier for them both. But, with her as his navigator, they got lost a number of times. He was beside himself and angrily, he'd swiped the list from her so that he could read it himself. They ended up arguing all the way to his cousin's home and if that incident wasn't enough, when he was employed as a long distance driver he'd be paid directly into their bank account, but it caused a problem. She could never budget properly and even with the amount of money he'd received, there was never enough left in their bank account. As far as he was concerned, she'd messed that up too and the red bills would be in a pile whenever he returned home. In his frustrations, he never made her forget and so took over in operating the home even when he wasn't at home.

As for Mrs Benjamin, when she was very young she'd lost her parents in a car crash and was raised in foster care. By the time she'd reached eighteen years of age, she left the home to fend for herself. She was lucky since she was raised in a loving and caring foster home but like Mr Benjamin, she wasn't a strong reader either but loved art and was very good at it and when Ismay was younger, she'd helped her with her art projects. But as Ismay grew older, she lost interest. It was also in the early years when her and Ismay's relationship had been good, and when they'd spent a lot of time together but even then, she could never understand her daughter and always felt she was different. With Ismay being opinionated, confident and doing what she wanted to do, it caused a lot of problems in the home. Ismay would always talk back and when Mr Benjamin left, things got steadily worse.

Everything, both she and Mr Benjamin had helped to build, was now shattered. It had been difficult for both parents, not knowing which way to turn or how to fix it, yet, even with all this knowledge and experience, both parents still had no idea of what was yet to come.

Chapter 5

It was Ismay's 21st birthday but she was more like going on 40. She'd always acted older than her actual age and would worry about her life. She often wondered if there was more it had to offer than what she was currently experiencing.

As the years passed, she was finding life to be very challenging and having left school without any qualifications it was hard for her to get a job, so she spent most of her days going out with her friends, partying or eating out, and whenever she was at home, she'd only watch television – doing nothing else. Ismay struggled with her self-confidence and even her bright nature seemed to be fading. She was at a crossroads, uncertain of where she wanted to go or even how to get there. In addition, her relationship with her parents was very strained and this showed in the home especially as she still lived with her mother, who, in turn, complained about her not finding a job and watching television all day.

It was on her birthdays and the only time they came together as a family, something they chose to keep doing unless or until Ismay had decided otherwise. A lovely restaurant in the city was where they would celebrate since Ismay loved it and as eating out was one of the things she thoroughly enjoyed. Plus, contrary to everything else, she still loved when her parents and herself spent time together; the warmth of togetherness, no worries or thinking about life, replaced by a sense of being in a special moment.

They entered the restaurant together. It was bright yellow with a tall ceiling and massive windows and had a Victorian layout with paintings hanging from the walls and drawings of up and coming artists. Her mother selected the restaurant knowing her daughter would love its artistic side and because of her love for drawing and painting. A waiter showed them to their table.

"This place is gorgeous," said Ismay as they took their seats, "I love it here, Mum."

The word love wasn't an expression which came from Ismay much and Mrs Benjamin smiled. While looking over the menu, they decided on what to eat, Mrs Benjamin began to chuckle while reading it.

"Remember Ismay, how you used to say "steak", you'd always say "aek". Even up to 8-years-old you'd say "aek" then quickly change it to "steak"."

They laughed so hard Ismay's eyes watered. "Well Mum believe it or not I still say it."

The laughter was so loud that the other customers began to look over, that didn't stop the Benjamin's and their laughter and caused the other patrons to smile.

"Ismay what about when you used to call Epping Forest - "effing forest" - leaving out the p's and that was just the other day?"

They all laughed and Ismay nearly fell from her chair. Her incorrect pronouncing of words was difficult for her and nobody knew why but it helped lighten the evening since they hadn't laughed this way for a long time. Looking over, her father stared at both his daughter and her mother - his ex-wife - wondering how things could've gotten so bad, where laughter no longer existed within the family. Now, years later, both he and Mrs Benjamin were just tolerating each other and with Ismay, there was a feeling that nobody understood her.

They ordered their food and drinks while chatting away, enjoying themselves and each other. Suddenly, Mrs Benjamin thought it was a good time to give Ismay her gift. "Ismay, since this is your special birthday, we chose to get you a gift from the both of us."

Ismay squealed, gladly receiving the gift. "What is it?"

"Well if you opened it, you'd find out," answered her father.

The gift was in a big red box, a blue bow wrapped around it. She had no clue as to what it might be and the excitement of not knowing bubbled in her as she undid the bow and opened it. Her eyes opened wide in surprise.

"Oh my, it's an art and craft set!" smiled Ismay. "Thank you so much."

She gave both her parents a kiss on their cheeks, before returning her attention to the box. Everything she needed for painting and drawing was in there: synthetic brushes, acrylic ink, water paint, brushes, pencils, canvases with wooden frames and a table-top easel. Smiling, both her parents hoped this would be the start of Ismay's journey in pursuing a career. At one time, they'd both believed she'd be the next Vincent Van Gogh. They knew that even though Ismay was extremely artistic, creative and could literally draw or make anything, she seemed to lack motivation and self-esteem, and, in their own way both parent's felt that they'd failed Ismay by not persevering with her and her talent.

They ordered dessert and Ismay had her favourite - apple crumble and ice cream with a dash of strawberry syrup trickled on the side. While they ate, her mother asked a question, "Ismay how's the job hunting going?"

"Oh Mum, please don't start, we're having such a lovely time. Why bring something like that up now?"

Her mother flinched. Nobody knew when it was the best time to ask Ismay such questions. "Sorry dear, I thought this would be a great time to discuss something like this," she hesitated, "have you thought about selling your paintings?"

"What? My paintings that are half done and not good enough?" Ismay shrugged, with her everything was always half done and whenever she felt this way, she'd be impatient, never returning to complete it.

"Ok guys that's enough," said Mr Benjamin as he called to the waiter. "Excuse me waiter, can I have the bill please. I think we should call this dinner to an end while things are still going so well."

"I agree," said her mother, awkwardly. Her father paid and they put on their coats, readying to leave.

"I'm not coming back home Mum," Ismay suddenly said. "I think I'll take a little stroll and see you later, thank you both I do appreciate the gift and for always being there for me, even though I know I can be very hard work at times." She giggled while her parents chuckled.

"Well, what can I say," stated her father, "we wouldn't have you any other way and just want you to be happy in life."

"I know Dad but I feel I need to do this on my own," replied Ismay.

They walked through the restaurant to the exit and Ismay stopped to look at some beautiful paintings on the walls. "You guys go on without me, I just need to use the toilet, I'll see you later."

With her parents gone, Ismay turned to the waiter who'd served their table. "Hi, sorry to bother you, may I speak to the manager please?"

"Ok, just a moment I'll get her for you." He departed to get the manager. A woman, dressed in a blue suit, white shirt and bright orange shoes, returned. Her shoes were so bright, Ismay noticed them right away. They nearly hurt her eyes.

"Can I help you?" The woman asked.

"Yes, I wanted to know the procedure on how to get paintings on the walls."

"For you?"

"Yes."

"Do you have a painting portfolio?" She asked.

"Oh, yes I do," Ismay answered.

"Ok, great. Bring it in and we can see what we can do."

"Thank you so much," Ismay said, offering and shaking her hand. As she walked away, she had the biggest smile on her face and outside the restaurant she shouted as loud as she could: "YES...!"

Ismay knew she had no painting portfolio ready but this was her chance to make a difference in her own life and so she promised herself, she'd go home and start painting straight away. Placing headphones over her ears, she tapped an icon on her phone and started to sing while walking down the street: *"I'm so happy.........."*.

For the first time in a very long while, she finally felt alive. Things were beginning to look up. She thought about what painting she'd start with; should she use her stack of unfinished paintings or begin afresh, creating a new lease of life. She grinned and believed that if her energy had been in a negative place, then whatever she placed her hands on would also become negative; yet if she'd a positive one, then only a positive outcome would appear. Elated, she began to run, she needed to get home as fast as she could, to tell her Mum the great news and immediately start to paint.

Smiling and laughing, she raced down the street. Rounding a corner and crossing the street... there was a sudden and loud bang...

Chapter 6

People ran over to the car crushed against a lamp post and someone shouted, "Call an ambulance, someone's trapped underneath!"

"Can you hear me love?" Another person called, bending over a figure on the ground. There was no answer or movement. A man, the driver, was staggering from the damaged vehicle, he was shaking, voice trembling, "She...she just came out of...of nowhere. Let me see if I...I can move the car."

"No!" Someone yelled. "We're not sure what injuries she might have. An ambulance is on its way."

A crowd quickly gathered around the young lady and it became bigger and within ten minutes an ambulance arrived. The two ambulance crew members rushed over, hastily approaching the still body. One member dropped his medical kit and knelt beside Ismay, checking her pulse, lifting her eyelids and shining a penlight into her eyes. "Hi, can you hear me? What's your name?"

Placing an oxygen mask over her mouth, he turned to his colleague. "Johnny, radio in for the air ambulance, we may not have much time. She seems to be falling in and out of consciousness, and her breathing is irregular."

Johnny walked a few feet away and talked into his radio, calling for an air ambulance.

****

A strange but bright light appeared. A kind of energy, with beautiful upbeat light-yellow, white and light blue colours. It waved through the air and within it was a darker-yellow figure.

"Where am I?" Asked Ismay, she was floating. She was…nothing but air.

"You're in the Temple of Consciousness," replied the entity; Ismay smiled. She felt a warm and total bliss coming from it.

"Why am I here?" She asked.

"You're here to be reminded of your journey on earth, an illusion that you chose to experience."

"I don't know about my life on earth, no one seems to understand me."

"That's because you don't understand yourself," the energy responded. "I found it to be quite lonely and I saw you trying to live up to other people's expectations. Remember, Ismay, you've been judged on things you do, say or don't do. Would you believe me if I told you, you chose your entire experience on earth?"

"Really?" Ismay queried. "I'm sure I wouldn't have chosen to leave school without any qualifications, unable to get a job, people misunderstanding me, never having the patience to complete things, having no self-confidence, coming from a broken home. The list goes on and on...."

"Would you believe me if I told you the real school is your experience on earth, the school of your earthly life. It's only for a time and you must make the most of it."

"But how?" Ismay asked, the light brightening each time she asked.

"By listening to your intuition, it speaks to you, it gives you all the answers you need while you're there. So far you've not been listening, you just moan, soak or disregard what people have to say to you. Every single person who enters your life is there to teach you, heal you, love you and hurt you. A balance you've chosen. If you start to open up, stop taking life too seriously and just enjoy your adventure. And you'll begin to see, hear, taste and feel the beauty of life."

The energy's colours began to flicker, changing to gold. A warm glow came over Ismay as it surrounded her entire soul; a feeling of contentment and pureness of love, she once thought she could never obtain.

"Why do I feel so at peace, so loved and so centred?" She asked.

"The feeling you've entered is the love of the all, the love of us. I want you to never forget this feeling for when you return to earth, it's this feeling that'll guide you on your journey - the feeling of us."

"What do you mean by 'us'?" said Ismay.

"Let me explain it this way," the energy continued, "the whole universe is made of energy, the energy of love and the energy of us, everything is not separated which means we're all one. That is what I mean by 'us'. Ismay, our time is running out, we don't have long before you have to go."

But Ismay didn't want to leave. "I don't want to go back. Why can't I stay here?"

"Because your earthly life is to continue, remember this part of your journey, you chose to have this experience, then go back."

"Can I ask one last question?"

"Of course."

"Will I have a purpose to complete?"

"Oh yes indeed, we're going to have a ball unravelling it and it won't be easy. There'll be a lot of physical and emotional hurt but remember within the hurt a beautiful flower is there to blossom. Your purpose is within you, for you to share and make a difference."

Slowly, the light began to fade and bit-by-bit, it turned into a pixel of colours before disappearing into nothingness.

****

Ismay lay in a hospital bed, her parents by her bed side. She'd been in a coma for three weeks not knowing whether she'd live or die. The doctors having also prepared her parents for the worse. Mrs Benjamin would never forget the moment when she'd received the phone call. Her heart felt like someone had tugged it from her chest and crumbled it into little pieces and she couldn't breathe. The pain and hurt was just too much for her to bear and tears had rolled down her face until she could no longer see. Like they were doing now, and staring at Ismay, she prayed: *"Please God not my only child...."*

On hearing the urgent voice over the phone, she wasn't sure how or where to begin when she needed to tell Mr Benjamin. Ever so slowly, she'd walked over to her phone and dialled his number.

"Hello!" Mr Benjamin hardly ever heard from his ex-wife and wondered why now. A tense feeling had come over him when he heard the sobbing. "What's wrong, is it Ismay?"

He became numb, sat on a chair and inhaled deeply since within him, he knew something had happened to Ismay.

He whispered, "Talk to me, what happened?"

She gave him the bad news and he started crying. "Ismay was in an accident earlier. A car knocked her over. They're rushing her by air ambulance to the hospital..."

Mrs Benjamin's voice raced. She was inhaling and exhaling at the same time while she spoke.

"Ok calm down Betty, I'm on my way. Which hospital is she in?" asked Mr Benjamin, anxiously. He needed to be doing something.

"The Crosstain Hospital."

"Ok, I'm on my way now."

He put down the phone and for a few seconds sat quietly, the tears streaming down his face as he thought how or why something like this would happen to his daughter on her birthday. Trembling, he began to pray: *"Please Lord, make our Ismay be ok...."*

As he sat crying, he knew he needed to be strong for the family but wasn't sure how he could be, but, yet, no matter what, he knew his Ismay needed him and grabbing his coat from a coat rack, he rushed out the door.

A week later...while Ismay's parents were by her bedside, a doctor walked in.

"Hello Mr and Mrs Benjamin, Ismay's condition has immensely improved so we're going to try and wake her today."

Holding her hands to her chest, Mrs Benjamin smiled, tears of joy clouding her eyes. "Is this good news doctor, we weren't sure...she had so many major injuries..."

The doctor replied, "There's still a long road of recovery for Ismay. However, she's responding well to the medication we've given her.

Until she wakes, we'll not know for sure how bad her injuries are, everybody heals differently and since the car crashed into her side, breaking her lower pelvis, we're uncertain how this will affect her walking. At a later date, Ismay will need another operation on her lower pelvis. So we'll just have to wait and see."

Mrs Benjamin smiled, she was just grateful Ismay was alive. "We don't care if she can walk or not, we're just grateful she is here. Anything else we can work with once our daughter is alive."

Mr and Mrs Benjamin looked at each other, tears filled their eyes and for a moment they didn't care about what had happened in the past. Embracing each other warmly, they gave thanks that their only child would probably be fine.

Chapter 7

For a few weeks, Mr and Mrs Benjamin waited intensely, praying everyday Ismay would wake from her coma and each day they'd sit by their daughter's bed, with one of her hands in one of theirs. A few machines, with wires attached to her body, hummed and bleeped.

"These past weeks have felt like years," Mrs Benjamin stated. "We've read and sang to her and I've done drawings just to let her know we're there for her. It has taken a lot out of us but I wouldn't change it for anything. It's been good having you here."

"I know, I feel the same way," Mr Benjamin said, nodding, "You've been great, going home and returning by 6am. I don't know how you do it but don't worry she'll be fine. I can feel it."

It was late afternoon, when they'd moved into the waiting area and a doctor arrived to see them. He strolled over, a small smile on his face. "I've some great news," he paused, smile becoming brighter, "Ismay woke up from her coma. She's very tired right now and we needed to place a tube down her throat, to clear her airway. So, she cannot talk just about now. However, she's acknowledging people by blinking with her eyes."

Mrs Benjamin jumped to her feet and didn't even wait for the doctor to finish talking. "...Can we go and see her now?"

"Of course you can." The doctor said, grinning.

Mr Benjamin chased after his ex-wife as they rushed down the corridor, bumping into patients, nurses and other doctors; apologising as they went. But they just didn't care, all they wanted to do was see their daughter. Ismay.

"Sorry, sorry my daughter is awake!" shouted Mrs Benjamin, after colliding with a doctor.

Reaching the room door, she gently opened the door, so as not to make any noise. Both Mr and Mrs Benjamin walked in. Ismay looked the same but peaceful and asleep. A nurse was by one of the machines, studying some flashing numbers.

The nurse smiled. "It's ok, come in she's just sleeping from all the medication. She's doing just fine and has moved her eyelids and nodded her head whenever you ask her questions."

Mrs Benjamin dropped into a vacant seat and began to shake and cry. She laughed nervously. Thoughts rushed through her mind. She didn't know how soon Ismay would wake or whether she'd be brain damaged, have memory-loss of who she was or even be able to talk. At that exact moment, she felt Mr Benjamin's hand softly hold hers.

"Don't worry my dear, Ismay is alive and will be ok. We both have to be strong since she needs us right now."

"I know, this has been very hard for all of us and she'll need us more than ever before."

Mr Benjamin agreed. "We'll make sure she's alright."

That night Ismay didn't wake and her parents left the hospital late in the night, to return early in the morning.

The follow morning arrived...and Mr and Mrs Benjamin hurried back to the hospital to make sure Ismay was fine. As they walked into her room they saw that she was awake, a tube in her mouth was connected to one of the humming machines. Smiling, Mrs Benjamin placed one hand on her daughter's and using her other, stroked her hair. It was soft to the touch.

"You gave us such a scare my love," stated Mrs Benjamin, "don't you ever do that to us again. How're you feeling?"

Ismay grinned, pointed to her throat and shook her head. Mr Benjamin laughed, indeed Ismay was back.

The doctor suddenly walked in.

"May I speak to you outside Mr and Mrs Benjamin?"

"Of course." Mrs Benjamin replied while Mr Benjamin nodded. They walked outside, smiling, hoping for better news. They headed into the waiting area, where the doctor showed them to some seats.

"We've some news. Ismay has made a great recovery, to our surprise. She still needs surgery on her broken pelvis but that can't be done as yet," he paused, staring intently at Mr and Mrs Benjamin, "her blood has become infected and we need to treat that first."

"What! What do you mean? How could that've happen?" Mr Benjamin asked, eyes wide.

"At present, we're uncertain. However, we're treating it."

Mrs Benjamin grabbed her ex-husband's hands and squeezed them tightly. He squeezed back, reassuring her. Worry lines crossed their foreheads.

He asked, "What does that mean?"

"I…I don't understand," Mrs Benjamin stammered, close to crying, "does…does this mean she won't be able to walk until she has the operation?"

"Yes, I'm afraid so," the young doctor answered but he then brightened, "but there's good news. If Ismay continues to progress as well as she has, she'll be able to go home and return for her surgery. So don't give up hope, there's still work to be done and we want to make sure she's one hundred percent better."

Mrs Benjamin closed her eyes and whispered, "Thank you Doctor. Thank you! We just want our daughter home."

"Yes, thank you Doctor, for everything you've done. We'll look after her," added Mr Benjamin, taking the doctor's hand and shaking it. "We just want her to be better, doing what she loves, living her life. This has been hard for us."

The doctor nodded. "I know and we'll do all we can to make sure she does get better."

"Can we share the news with her?" Mrs Benjamin asked.

"Of course," said the doctor, "we still have a long way to go but with time and patience everything should be fine. And tell her, that she's one brave young lady and we're very proud of her progress."

"Thank you," Mr Benjamin said. "We will and we're so proud of her too."

Leaving the doctor, they walked down the corridor and back to Ismay's room, wondering how she'd take the news of being unable to walk for a while. They knew of her impatience and not listening to anyone, at times, and worried how she'd cope with this new, upsetting experience to come.

Mrs Benjamin bent over her daughter, softly stroking her hair. "Hi Ismay, how you doing sweetheart? We've some good news for you." She paused for a moment. "You should be able to come home soon, my darling."

Seated to one side, Mr Benjamin smiled encouragingly. "Yes, baby, you can come home soon but they still need to treat you for a blood infection you have. So the surgery for your pelvis won't be for now," he hesitated, holding onto one hand, gently rubbing it, "which means you'll have to use a wheelchair to get around just for a while.

Don't worry I've already spoken to your mother and I'll take sometime off work to help look after you. Everything will be fine."

Opening and closing her mouth, Ismay tried to talk. It was difficult and so she pointed to a pen and paper on a nearby stand - a serving tray lay empty beside them.

"Oh you want to write something, Ismay?" asked Mrs Benjamin, grabbing the pen, paper and tray, and giving them to her.

Slowly, Ismay picked up the pen, her hand shook uncontrollable for a brief while before it steadied. She wrote on it and pointed at the paper for her mother to pick it up.

Mrs Benjamin read out aloud: "*Love is everything...*"

Both, her parent's stared at each other in confusion. Mr Benjamin shrugged. Mrs Benjamin responded.

"What do you mean, love?" Mrs Benjamin asked. "We don't understand." Ismay pointed to the paper for it to be placed in her hand. Her mother did so. She started writing again, before returning it to her mother.

I'll be fine.

She put the pen down and smiled while nodding her head. Her parents stared at each other, then at their daughter, returning her smile. Mrs Benjamin returned to stroking Ismay's hair. "Don't worry my love, we know you'll be just fine."

As the weeks passed and after her various hospital trip check-ups, Ismay was becoming stronger and stronger. By now, she could sit in and use her wheelchair like an expert user and one of the first things she'd asked to do was to go into the garden. She wished to feel the air of life, the soft breeze touching her skin, see the blue sky and hear the birds sing. It became a habit for her.

A nurse wheeled her to a nearby leafy tree. "I'll be fine here," Ismay said.

"Will you be fine to return on your own?" The nurse asked.

"Yes, I'll be fine."

She looked through the tree's leaves and towards the sky, taking a deep breath. Gently, she placed her hands on the tree, appreciating its trunk's roughness. Closing her eyes, she inhaled and exhaled deeply, the smell of the tree, feeling its energy breathe through her touch. Quietly, she gave thanks for getting another chance at her earthly life. That was how she saw it. She hadn't told anyone about her near-death-experience after the accident since she wasn't sure how her family would take it or if they'd even believe her. Not that she needed anyone to really believe her, so for the time being, she figured she'd keep her experience a secret - between herself and the Universe. Eventually, it was time for her to return home, to await the surgery on her pelvis.

Chapter 8

Four weeks later...Ismay's parents struggled looking after her. With her being bound in a wheelchair, it wasn't easy for them and they hadn't counted on or realised how difficult it'd be. Helping to wash, clothe and feed her, take her on her daily strolls and attending to her every need, was becoming stressful. They even gave her a bell so that she could press whenever she needed their assistance, and Ismay wasn't afraid to use it for any little thing she wanted. Because of her constant demands, her parents moved her room from upstairs to the living room, downstairs and swopped the living room to upstairs. At times and when she was lying on her bed, Ismay would be in great pain. It'd be so severe, she'd grip her pillow and bite into it until her teeth made holes in the cotton. But she never made her parents to know how much pain she was in, so she'd embraced it by screaming and sobbing into the pillow's fluffiness. She had good and bad days and whenever things got really bad she'd cry herself to sleep, wondering why she felt low. It was at these times that she'd remember what she was told by the bright energy.

One morning she woke up and for some reason the day felt different. She didn't know why or how but when she looked out of the living room window, the sun was in a blue sky and the air smelt of roses. She stared into the clouds and thought: *Wow! The clouds look like they're talking to me with a piercing eye look at me...*

She went to the other side of the room and from a cupboard, took out a drawing pad and pencil. Returning to the window, she started to draw. The clouds looked as if they were smiling and a warm feeling came from them - a deep and friendly energy. She began to draw and for the first time in a very long while, she felt at complete peace.

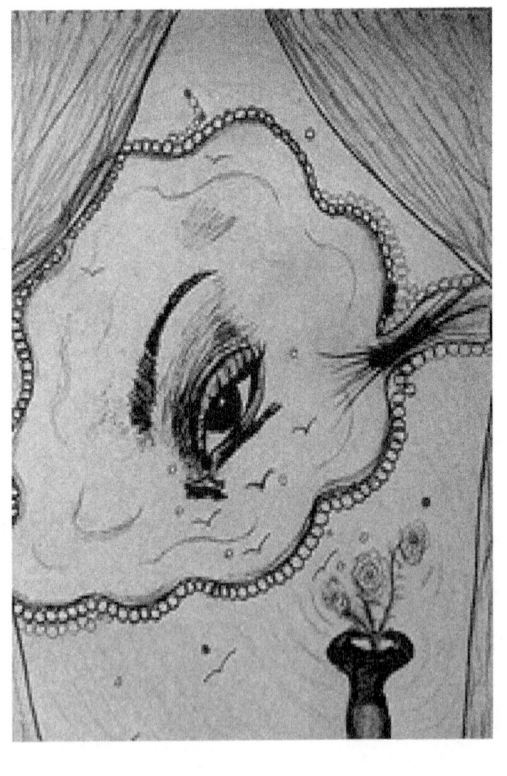

Entering the room, Mrs Benjamin saw her and smiling, asked, "Ismay are you ready for your lunch?"

"No, I'm not hungry. Plus, I just need to finish this drawing."

Mrs Benjamin stared. "Oh, wow. Ok love, just let me know when you're ready."

Slowly she left the room, surprised to see her daughter getting back into drawing and not wanting to make a fuss, she acted like she'd never noticed.

The days went by and Ismay drew and painted more and more. Her art was giving her a sense of peace, joy and most of all making her think of something else than her constant pain. But being outdoors, the drawings of nature made her feel alive for the first time in years. She loved it. Once outside, a lot of thoughts kept going through her mind as she drew her future and the past but, always, there was one thing that kept popping up.

While she sat in a wide and beautiful park near her home, sketching a lake with trees along a pathway, she wondered why she'd never understood or connected with reading and writing; however, she loved anything creative. She wasn't just good at art but anything where she needed to use her hands like making clothes, doing hair and knitting. It was at those times she felt free and having her freedom was very important to her. She'd never connected with her academic studies in any shape or form and as she sat in the park drawing it slowly came to her: *Ok, let me try and draw how writing and reading makes me feel, this might just help me understand why my life has turned out the way it has.*

Closing her eyes, she breathed deeply until she began to visualise her studying back in her school days. At first, she was anxious, then, slowly, other emotions began to flow; from joy to pain to stillness. They surprised her since she'd thought she'd overcome her school days. Nonetheless, those feelings made her draw again and within an hour her vision was on a piece of paper staring back at her. Tears welled in her eyes and the drops dripped onto the paper like drizzles of rain falling from the sky. She couldn't believe this was how she'd felt about school and studying all this time. She'd been afraid all her life and had felt like she was chained, trying to break free. She couldn't understand her feelings and as she sat in her wheelchair and moved along the lake to return to her home, there were many things for her to think about.

Chapter 9

A year went by and Ismay's surgery had been a great success and she, Mr and Mrs Benjamin celebrated by returning to her favourite restaurant. Finally, she was walking again and was starting to do things for herself, however, she still got very tired at times but, even with this challenge, she was grateful for her health. She was more than grateful that she could walk once again. As for her family, they were overjoyed with her recovery and the change that somehow seemed to have come over her. They saw it but were unable to understand much less explain it, so they dared not say a word and instead, were just thankful Ismay was alive.

Ismay's journey was changing right before her and her family's eyes.

One day, Mr Benjamin came to visit her, and she loved their chats. He'd never judged her but at the same time would still put forward his views on things. "Hello young lady, how are you today?"

They were in her room: Ismay lying on her bed, he seated on one side.

"I'm fine Dad, just working on finishing my paintings," said Ismay. "Dad there's something I would like to share with you?"

"Of course, my love."

"A thought came to me the other day of why I never liked school. There was a fear of reading and writing but I didn't know why. It felt like I was in chains. I can honestly say, for some reason I never connected with reading, writing or anything academic. I found them to be difficult and always have, that's why I didn't like school and never wanted to be there."

Her father looked at her but said nothing. He'd felt the same way about his growing up and pondered on whether to tell her he'd felt the same. The moment of silence between them wasn't uncomfortable like it had been once before.

"Look, I drew this last year when I was healing."

Her father stared at the detailed drawing. "That's amazing Ismay, why haven't you showed me this before?"

"I've done many drawings and paintings over the years. They've helped me through the pain and gave me the peace to look within and find myself, that was something I needed to do alone. I know it looked like I was being selfish and isolated but I remembered we come into this world alone and leave alone."

Mr Benjamin sat, staring at his daughter. He'd never heard her speak this way before and was astonished. "We've seen a change in you and don't think we haven't. We felt it be best to leave you to whatever that changing was but we're very proud of how you've dealt with everything you've been through. You're a brave and strong young lady."

Ismay reached over and got some more artwork she'd been working on. She showed her father. Mr Benjamin was surprised.

"Wow Ismay, you've been busy," he chuckled, "these are beautiful."

"You know what I haven't shared with you?" Ismay smiled. "You remember on my 21st Birthday when we celebrated at the restaurant with those wonderful paintings on the walls?"

"Yes, of course I remember," said her father. "How can I forget? Your accident was the same day."

"Well that day when you and mum left, I went to talk to the manager. She was willing to see my artwork, I was so excited that I tried to rush home to tell you guys and begin working on my art, not realising I wouldn't get there."

Mr Benjamin was in shock. Ismay had never shared this before with him.

"Why didn't you say anything?" He asked.

"It wasn't the right time, what I do know is that it was part of my journey. It needed to happen to me to get me where I am today. It hasn't been easy, however, I can now see the beauty within it."

Mr Benjamin looked at his daughter. She'd never ever spoken the way she was now and as much as he knew Ismay had her own mind, this time felt different. She wasn't just knowing and owning her own mind but completing the actions, doing new things. He sat in awe, listening to his daughter.

Ismay continued, "Dad, I'm not the same person I was before the accident, the only way I can explain it, is to say I feel like the old me died for a new birth to arrive. I know, that sounds silly," she laughed, nervously.

Mr Benjamin grinned, "No, not at all I always knew there was something special about you from the day you were born. We - me and your mother - may not understand but we're here for you nevertheless."

"I know you both have always been there for me even though at times I couldn't see it but now I'm awake and that's the main thing," Ismay agreed. She went into a side drawer and took out another piece of paper, and showed to her father. "Look, I wrote this in my groundhog day state, feeling like my life was just repeating itself day-in-day-out while I was in pain. Not until there was that lightbulb moment."

Mr Benjamin began to read...

I am here in this light,

The light of my home,

Everything is open and free for

the energy to pass through,

I feel the Most High with delight in my home I call home,

I often asked why did my home often feel so dark?

HE/SHE would answer.... you kept forgetting to turn me on.

After a few silent minutes, her father inhaled before saying, "Oh wow Ismay, this is so beautifully and delicately written. I didn't know you wrote poetry. I'm really shocked."

"Well there you go Dad, that's something else you never knew about me."

They both laughed.

"If you don't mind Dad, can we finish this conversation another time, I've to get ready to buy something?"

"Ok...right, going to buy anything nice?"

"Yes, I'm going to buy a seed plant."

"Wow, ok that's different," Mr Benjamin said. "May I ask why?"

"Well as we know a seed is an embryonic plant enclosed in a protective outer covering, the formation of the seed is the process of reproduction. This process is what I've been going through within the past year or so. I've been feeling very blocked and couldn't find a way out, not realising I was growing and learning while going through the process. The seed plant will mirror who I am today. Me getting out of the rut, but looking to grow and learn at the same time. Remember when I used to pick flowers for you from the adventure playground when I was younger, I've always loved flowers."

"Yes I remember," said her father. He was beside himself, gobsmacked and speechless unsure of what to say. The young lady before his eyes was definitely the *new* Ismay. "Ok, my dear you go and enjoy."

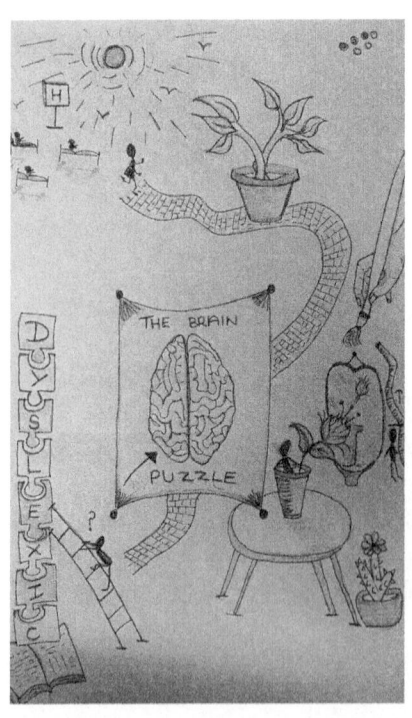

Ismay walked down the street looking for a flower shop. She wasn't sure what seed she'd buy but felt to go with the flow. Walking across a zebra crossing to get to the other side, she came upon a shop, went in and looked around. She'd no clue what seed to go for, then, suddenly, she saw some rose seeds. She always loved roses and felt this would be the ones. She purchased a few, bought a plant pot and soil to go with the seeds and headed out. She thought that when she reached home, she'd keep the seeds in her room. On the way she saw a poster on the window:

Do you find reading and writing challenging?

Do you miss out words and letters when writing?

Are you more of a creative thinker?

If YES to all of the above, this Dyslexia Awareness workshop maybe for you!

DYSLEXIA, Ismay mumbled: *Interesting, my answer is yes to all of these questions.* She knew very little of what dyslexia was and just thought it just affected people with special education needs. However, that wasn't her since she could answer yes to all the questions. She began to wonder was this the reason why she'd never connected with school or studying. Taking her phone, she took down the date and time of the workshop. She knew she'd need to go to find out more as this could be a piece of the puzzle that'd been missing all this time in her life.

When Ismay got home, her mother was in the living room watching television. "Excuse me Mum, do you know anything about dyslexia?"

"Not really Ismay, I believe it's people that find reading and writing difficult, why do you ask?"

"No reason." She called as she ran upstairs to her room. Things were beginning to reveal themselves to her, now she couldn't wait for next month to arrive.

Chapter 10

The morning arrived for Ismay to attend the dyslexia training. She got herself ready from very early, to make sure she'd be on time. She didn't know what to expect. Nonetheless, she was excited and butterflies buzzed around in her stomach like little flickers of light trying to jump out.

Arriving at the venue, she entered the building and walked along a hallway, signs pointed to where the workshop was being held. She headed to a set of stairs to her left, noticing how white the walls were with its drawings and paintings. She followed the signs to Room 206.

Ismay entered the room and saw some people already sitting, in a half circle. A woman said, "Hello! Hello, come in it's nice to meet you, my name is Zoe, the facilitator for this workshop. Please take a seat and help yourself to refreshments on the side table, over there."

"Thank you," Ismay said, smiling.

"We're just waiting for some more people to arrive then we'll start."

"Ok." Ismay started looking around. Suddenly, she felt a bit uncomfortable and thought: *What am I really doing here? This isn't even for me I might as well go? I could just say I'm going to the toilet and shoot out the back.*

The negative thoughts came until she heard... "...Ok, we're going to begin."

There was no escaping now and she figured if it wasn't saying much she'd stay for just about an hour. The facilitator started by introducing herself again, explained her journey with dyslexia and how she became to have her own company running workshops about it. Ismay sat in shock while listening to her story and she began to understand and realise that anyone could be dyslexic. Sometimes people didn't even know they were even dyslexic!

There and then as she sat and listened to Zoe, she knew she'd be staying for the entire workshop. The day was long with Ismay learning things about dyslexia she would've never thought of; the facilitator explained about the brain and how dyslexia was a neurological condition. She spoke about the different signs of dyslexia and how it could affect a person academically and creatively too. She said that dyslexia could be genetic and so could be passed down from parents. She broke down the dyslexia family and said that at times could overlap - *dyscalulia, dysgraphia, dyspraxia, ADHD* and *Autism*. The list was so long Ismay almost found it difficult to keep up with her notetaking but realised this too was also one of the dyslexia traits: writing slow and unable to keep up and at the sametime absorb the information; multi-tasking definitely wasn't her thing.

As she sat there, all of this fascinated Ismay. She couldn't believe it as she listened to Zoe and the other participants, she related to absolutely every single trait. I don't understand, I've all of these traits but how can this be? She asked herself and throughout the workshop she kept quiet and just listened, not participating much but taking everything in.

After the workshop had finished Ismay went over to Zoe. "Excuse me, can I just ask you a question?"

"Of course you can, fire away."

"How do you know if you are dyslexic?"

"A very good question," she said, "by the way you're free to call me Zoe."

"Ok," smiling, Ismay nodded.

"Now, dyslexia can come in so many forms and show itself in different ways, so every individual will have their own unique trait," Zoe caught herself and laughed. "Oh sorry my love, I'm going off on one instead of just answering you. See, that's part of my dyslexia."

They both laughed.

"Now, are you asking for yourself?" Zoe asked.

"Well yes, I've just realised most of the traits you were explaining I seem to have, I also hated writing and reading at school and never connected well throughout my whole school experience"

"Is there anyone in your family who has the traits?"

"I'm not sure to be honest."

"That'll be your starting point. Go and find out, after which you could get a dyslexia assessment to confirm if you are."

Ismay laughed, she couldn't believe what she was hearing. "Wow, I didn't know there was an assessment. How much does it cost and who does it?"

"I'm an assessor and can do it for you," Zoe said as she walked to the other side of the table, handing Ismay a dyslexia handbook. "Read this, there's great information in here. All you need to know and if you still think you may be dyslexic, feel free to give us a call. I can then book you in for an assessment. By the way if you're dyslexic welcome to the family of genesis!"

They both laughed. Ismay was so happy. Finally, there could be an answer to her lifelong problem.

"Thank you," she said, shaking Zoe's hand before leaving.

Ismay walked home, her thoughts on the workshop, she'd never been to any workshop where the facilitator explained something and drew the answer to show the meaning at the same time. Zoe's drawings were beautiful, detailed and unique, and Ismay loved the fact that she was dyslexic, had her own business, was creative, could draw, had a sense of humour and didn't care if the whole world knew she was dyslexic. Ismay thought, *now that's what I call confident.*

She reached home and went straight to her mother to share what she'd learnt about the workshop. Mrs Benjamin was in the kitchen, preparing dinner.

"Hi Mum," Ismay said.

"Hi my love, had a good day?"

"Yes, a very good one." She sat on a stool, watching her mother. "I went to a dyslexic workshop."

"Dyslexic?" Mrs Benjamin asked, quizzically. "Why would you go to a dyslexic workshop?"

Ismay smiled, "Because I think I may be one."

Her mother stared at her. "Why would you say that?"

"Because all the traits point that way and it makes sense as to why I hated school. Do you know how hard I found it to spell and read?"

"I didn't," stated her mother, "I just thought you were being lazy since you're a very bright young lady."

"I know," answered Ismay. "So is a dyslexic person they just learn differently, I've been learning all this today at a workshop I attended.

Dyslexia can also be genetic, so I wanted to ask you and Dad if you know if you've any of the traits."

"Well, what are the traits?"

"Difficulties with reading and writing, seeing words differently on paper, not knowing your right from your left, getting confused with directions, being unorganised, not being able to pronounce words easily, finding it difficult to absorb information and then having to write it down, the list goes on..."

Mrs Benjamin went quiet for a few moments before answering. "Hm...wow! That's a lot and if I really thought about it, both myself and your father may have some of those traits..."

Ismay interrupted her mother. "...Yes. You don't know what this'll mean if I am dyslexic. This would be the answer to the puzzle I've been looking for, why I hated school, why I gave up on myself, why I thought nobody understood me," she grabbed an apple from a fruit bowl and bit into it, "The lady who facilitated the workshop is also an assessor and she can do a dyslexia assessment on me. I really think I should get it done."

"Hmm...you think so?"

"Yes. I need to know."

"Ok, of course my love, if you're dyslexic *we* need to know." Mrs Benjamin emphasised.

They chatted while in the kitchen and through most of the evening, going through the family tree, trying to see where any similar traits were. As her mother recalled various relatives, they'd laugh. Then her mother reminded Ismay of when she tried to pronounce various words and something completing different came out.

For the next couple of weeks Ismay researched anything and everything she could about dyslexia and more and more she knew she saw herself with it. Finally, she was beginning to accept herself and what had caused so many problems in her life. There'd be a good reason as to why her behaviour was the way it had been when she was younger, now, she'd be happy to be dyslexic, if any assessment result came back saying so. She called Zoe to arrange for an appointment. At last she'd have a day to know what had pained her for so long.

Chapter 11

6 months later....the day for her assessment finally arrived and she went to the centre to meet Zoe. It didn't take long since the assessment was only for three hours. The session worked on her working memory, spelling, reading, grammar and overall academic knowledge. It wasn't easy and she found it challenging, and it showed she did have difficulties in these areas. After a while Zoe handed her the result. "Here you are Ismay, what do you think?"

Ismay stared at the piece of paper in her hand. She was unsure of how she really felt but holding the result with her name at the top and what it said, made her feel warm inside.

It came as no surprise to her that she was dyslexic and she embraced it, seeing the positive side. After leaving the centre and Zoe, Ismay went for a walk, just to think. Now she knew who she was, she needed to plan the rest of her life. Right there, she decided that she wanted to make a difference by helping other young people with the same condition, assisting them to acknowledge and embrace it. She not only wanted to give back to her community and be financially secure at the same time, she also wanted to support and provide for her family, especially after all she'd put them through.

Once she reached home, she created a ten-year visionboard by drawing everything she wanted to achieve - returning to studying, having her own business, supporting other people with their dyslexia and selling her paintings. Though this was a lot for her, she'd never been so organised or committed in her entire life. It just felt that now was the time.

With this renewed determination, the first thing she wanted to do was return to the restaurant where she'd celebrated her 21st birthday, to see if they were still willing to look at her artwork. She knew she was ready, especially after completing many paintings. She was also ready to study since this was a must for her, to prove to herself that she wasn't a failure and to make her parents finally proud of her achievements...*Wow*, she thought, *there's a lot to do, well I'd better get cracking...*

She arrived at the restaurant, walked in, and approached the reception. A young woman behind a low counter, smiled. It wasn't the same receptionist she'd met before. This one was much younger and wore glasses.

"Hi, is there anything I can help you with?"

"I just wondered if you were still taking up-and-coming artist's work?" Ismay asked, nervously, returning the smile.

"Oh yes we are, are you an artist? How long have you been drawing or painting?"

"Yes I am. Since I was little, I'm self-taught and use my dyslexic mind to guide me." Ismay caught herself, this was the first time she'd spoken out aloud about her condition to someone and it felt good. Really good.

The receptionist laughed, "Oh that's really weird, my daughter is dyslexic and loves to draw too. She's only ten and has one of her paintings up on the wall over there. Come on, let me show you."

She led Ismay to a hallway. She could hear crashing pans and sounds of a kitchen and saw signs for the Male and Female bathrooms, on the wall, in between the two rooms, was a lovely painting of a Lotus flower.

"That's so beautiful," said Ismay, in awe. "And you said she's just 10 years old?"

"Yes, indeed, I'm so proud of her, it's a shame she doesn't get those praises for her school work, she's struggling at the moment and I'm fighting with the school to get her some proper support," the receptionist said angrily, "it's been an ongoing battle...," Suddenly she stopped and smiled again. "But look at me talking away, sorry about that."

"No, not at all, thank you for showing me your daughter's painting, it's lovely," said Ismay. They returned to the reception.

"Ok look, bring your artwork, about five pieces if you can and price them up since some of our customers do sometimes come in and buy paintings."

"I'll see what I can do," Ismay answered, finding it difficult to contain her excitement. If she could've leapt into the air, she would've but, instead, she fought to remain calm.

"Ok great, thank you."

Ismay walked home. Strolling unconsciously, she reached a familiar spot. It was on the same stretch of road she had her mishap.

A sudden feeling of fear grabbed her but recalling the moment of the accident, she slowly began to feel different. She was in a good place and wasn't worried or scared anymore and her life was changing for the better and the more positive she was, the more confident she became. The thought about her near death experience and the moment she felt the Universe or God speak to her, she remembered it saying a beautiful flower would blossom. Well, her rose – the one she bought - was blossoming very well at home, so well in fact that she'd move it from her bedroom to the garden so that there was room for it to grow. Ismay grinned. A warm, loving feeling came over her and somehow she knew she was safe, being looked after and loved. Still up to that day, she hadn't told a soul about her experience and was unsure if she ever would.

It was later that week that Ismay returned to the restaurant with some of her artwork. The receptionist was totally delighted to see her and her work, she loved them.

"These paintings are beautiful, very different and unique. How long did you say you were painting for?"

"Since I was young but to be honest for the past couple of years I've committed myself to completing my work," Ismay explained, "I was in an accident and couldn't walk for a while so my art was really my saviour. It taught me patience and to have peace in my heart in order to heal."

The receptionist listened intensely. "How old are *you* young lady?"

Ismay laughed and she joined in. "Why?"

"You have an old soul, I can tell, my daughter is just the same."

"My mother always told me that since I was a little girl, so you may be right."

The receptionist smiled. "Let me take your art to the manager – Miss Hamilton - when she returns. She did say come back next week and she'll let you know if we'll accept your work."

Ismay was delighted, her grin shining on her face. "Ok, thank you."

Walking away from the restaurant, people who passed by kept smiling at her. Ismay would return an even brighter one.

She returned to the restaurant the following week. On entering, the receptionist showed her to Miss Hamilton's office; she looked just as young as the receptionist as she showed Ismay to a seat. She wore a smart navy blue business suit. The colour suited her. She was also new, different from the manager she'd met before.

"Hi Ismay," she said, offering her hand, "I loved your work so much, I was thinking. Could you do a painting for my home?"

Ismay tried her best to remain professional; it was a big effort just to stop herself from screaming. "That should be fine, do you know what painting you'd like and the size?"

"Not yet, will I be able to call you to discuss it?" Ismay nodded. "I definitely would love a painting done by you. You're a natural, I've seen many artists come here but there's something special about you. Mark my words, you're destined to be big."

"Thank you Miss Hamilton, that's really humbling to hear."

Offering her hand again, Miss Hamilton smiled. "It was great meeting you Ismay, leave your number with the receptionist."

As Ismay left the restaurant again, she felt like she could walk on air.

Within six weeks all five paintings were sold and Ismay had her first big pay day. She was buzzing with excitement and her family were delighted and for them, they still couldn't believe the change and confidence they saw. Now for her, the only way was up, she was growing. Eventually, with her painting being sold from the restaurant, she was able to give her mother housekeeping and rent, take her parents out to dinner, go out with friends and for the first time have fun without having to think about where the next penny would be coming from.

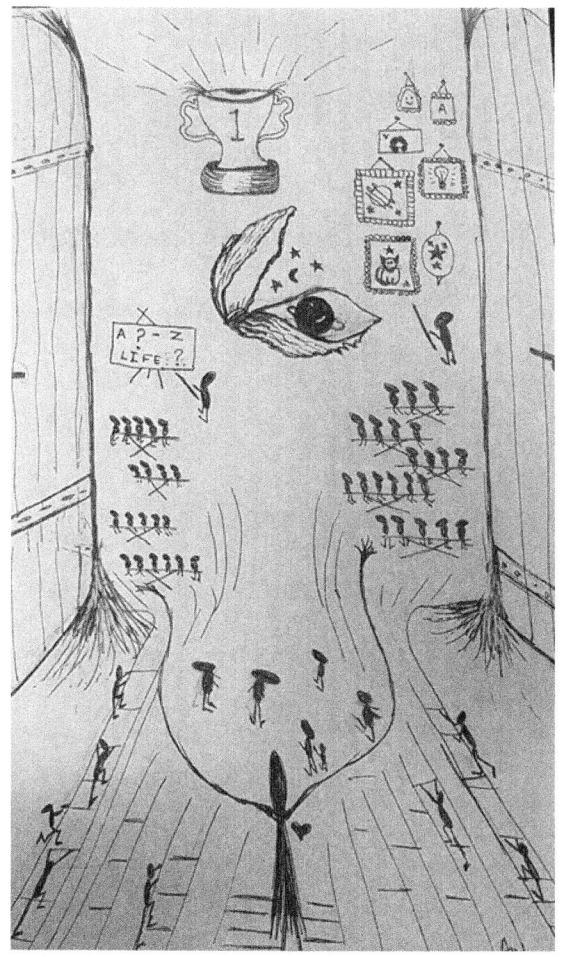

She returned to studying and this allowed her to pass English, Maths and Art, permitting her to attend university. It wasn't easy and Ismay needed to find ways to bring her creative mind over into an academic one, so that she could understand her assessments and be able to complete them. But there was a good thing, since she was dyslexic, she was able to gain extra support and time in her exams. However, she still felt the teachers weren't understanding her dyslexia and sometimes this meant her not receiving the right support. She'd still miss out words and sentences, found it difficult to absorb information when writing them down and in a way it could be understood, read long words but couldn't spell it, had trouble reading on white paper since the words would seem hazy or just go missing when she'd use a colour overlay.

This made Ismay think. There was a whole area that could be filled since nobody had looked to bring creativity and academia together, to support people who thought creatively. She also thought that people with dyslexia should be called creative thinkers since it wasn't a disability or a difficulty but a different way of learning. This started her planning and beginning her own business. She'd start with opening up a Saturday school for creative thinkers, where she taught spelling and reading through art, allowing children to be creative then adding in the academics. Ismay saw the idea in the film 'X Men' and it was about unique beings who were taken to a special school to be taught how to use their powers properly and responsibly. This was how Ismay saw dyslexia, if used properly it could change the world, she just needed to know where to begin.

With this new plan, she contacted Zoe to see if she could support her with guidance or advice. As she walked into the centre, she saw one of her paintings on the wall. A feeling of joy and pride flowed through her and as she sat, she couldn't take her eyes off her work. Zoe was soon down the stairs and saw her in the reception.

"Hi Ismay, how are you? I haven't seen you for such a long time." They hugged. "Let's go to the meeting room for a chat. Would you like some herbal tea?"

"No thank you," Ismay said as they made their way and sat in her comfortable office.

"So what can I do for you my lovely?"

"Well I've come up with an idea and wanted to know if you could help with some guidance or advice."

"Go ahead."

"I'm looking to open up a company where I can teach children academics in a creative way, this could be through art, dance acting etc. I feel the education system is not giving us creative thinkers the support we need. And I feel I can help make a difference."

"That sounds very interesting," Zoe agreed, "I think you're right. There's a gap in the education system and a change needs to happen. The more of us who come together to make that change, I feel in time it'll happen. What've you been doing for the past five years?"

"I returned to studying as I felt it was something I needed to do and complete, for myself. I now have my art degree…"

"Wow!" Zoe said excitedly, interrupting her, "Did you see your painting I brought on the wall outside?"

"Yes. Thank you for supporting me," Ismay said shyly, a small smile on her lips, "my paintings are selling well."

"I know. Why do you think I rushed and bought one before you made it much bigger and your prices went up!" They both laughed.

"I tell you what," Zoe added, "because I love how you've grown. You really remind me of myself when I was younger and I also love to help people who're motivated and believe in what they're doing. I can give you space right here at the centre for free while you get up and running."

Ismay was speechless. "Thank you so much."

"We'll need to write up a contract and other than that, you can start as soon as next week," before Zoe got up she added, "I believe in you Ismay, you may be the one who will really change the education system in a way that break cycles where us dyslexics are concerned....oh yes...sorry you call us creative thinkers now!"

Ismay laughed as she walked with Zoe out of the room. "Thanks again Zoe. I'm so speechless."

"No problems Ismay, see you soon."

Ismay left the centre, her hopes and dreams were now firmly in her hands.

Chapter 12

Ten years on...Ismay was now in her 30's and her life was moving so fast she wondered about her success. Her business was growing and she now had people working for her, listening to what she had to say as the boss. She no longer had any fear of expressing her opinions and believed in herself more now than ever before. But, her career had taken over her life which meant there'd been no time for children or settling down. Even though she loved children and loved helping them learn, something she'd never received as a child, there were times when she'd thought of having them but if time was running out, she knew she'd have to slow down for any such thing to happen.

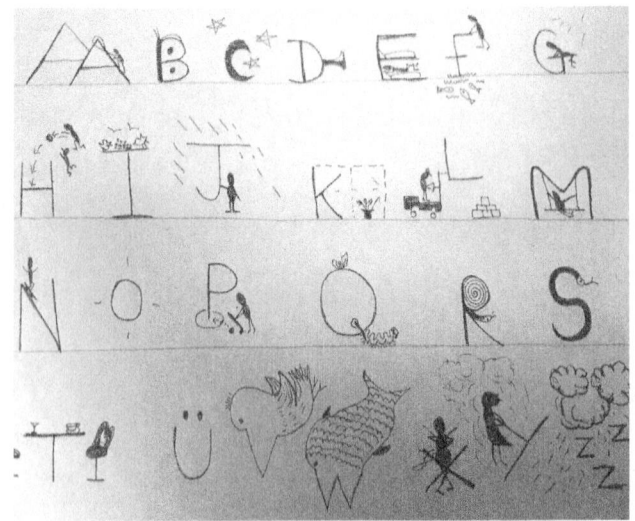

Ismay's business started from one room to her having her own centre. She now created projects which combined art, creativity and academics for children and young people, and children who weren't getting on in school could enrol and still complete their qualifications while using their creativity. For any young person who needed an assessment completed, Ismay would pass them onto Zoe's centre and their relationship remained and grew throughout the years. In her staff and volunteers, she took on people who were creative thinkers, for her it was about offering a chance to others unable to finish school or had no qualifications but had that natural entrepreneurism within them. Her experience enabled her to know so well what it felt like to be misunderstood or to have a condition and not know.

Eventually, Ismay was able to buy her first home and at twenty-five years of age, her dyslexia hadn't affected her ability with figures. She was very good with making money, saving and making sure things were in place so that she wouldn't really need to worry about the future. So when she brought her first house, she knew straight away she'd rent out the bottom two rooms so just in case business dried up, there'd still be money coming in. She leased the rooms only to female nurses and doctors since she preferred women, being a single woman herself. This worked well as she was still able to do her artwork and sell them while running a company.

Mr and Mrs Benjamin watched her progress and were so proud of her. Soon and as a family, they became much closer. In fact, Ismay's house was a couple of streets away from her mother's, so they saw a lot of her and whenever she had another idea or needed some advice from her parents, she'd go visit. Like today.

"Hi Mum, is Dad on his way?"

"Yes dear, what's this about. Is everything ok?" Her mother asked, concern in her voice.

"Yes of course, I just have a business idea and would like you and Dad's opinion."

Just then the doorbell rang. "Can you get that Ismay? I'm just popping to the loo," said Mrs Benjamin. Ismay opened the door. It was her father.

"Hi Dad." They hugged each other closely.

"Hi Ismay you look nice, that dress really suits you."

Ismay had on a green fitted knee length dress with single buttons down the back. She'd made it – the other thing she was good at.

"Thanks Dad." They walked into the kitchen where Mrs Benjamin was already seated around the kitchen table.

As Ismay and Mr Benjamin sat, she said, "Ok, the centre's going really well as you know and you know I love to recreate and continue to grow."

"Yep," said her father, "you're never still for too long."

They laughed.

"Exactly and that's part of the dyslexia because our brain is forever racing...that's why I wanted to move to the next level and create a cartoon on dyslexia."

"Wow, ok," said Ismay's mother, "do you know anything about directing a cartoon?"

"Not at all but you know me, I'll find out. You see, I don't really know of many cartoons that are addressing this topic and if we start presenting dyslexia in a creative way and positive light, from nursery age children, they'll automatically understand that it's ok to learn differently and children wouldn't need to be separated."

Her parents listened intensely and knew if anyone could do this, it'd be Ismay. The new Ismay did nothing by halves and definitely got things done.

"Go for it," said her father, "you've our blessing as always but please take it easy. You need to have time for yourself and rest since you're always on the go, we don't want you going before your time."

"Dad when it's my time nothing will be able to stop it. I don't know why, though but I feel I'll live into my 80's."

Her parents looked at each other as if to say 'here she goes again'. For the rest of the evening, they chatted before Ismay excused herself to go out with some of her friends.

Ismay's mindset allowed her to think 'outside the box' and this served her well in her later years. Sometimes, when she reflected on her past, she wondered how she'd done it, where she'd got the strength from, motivation and confidence to feel the fear and do it anyway. Along her journey, she'd met some wonderful people, who'd guided her, loved her, respected her and most of all believed in her. Some came into her life for just a short time then left but she realised they came to give her a helping hand, to give advice, so that she could learn from them or they learn before moving on. So she learnt that living in the moment was the real gift, a present not to take for granted.

It was 11pm and Ismay was on her computer finishing off some work. She was getting really tired and decided to finish up to what she'd call an early night. She came out of her office and walked along

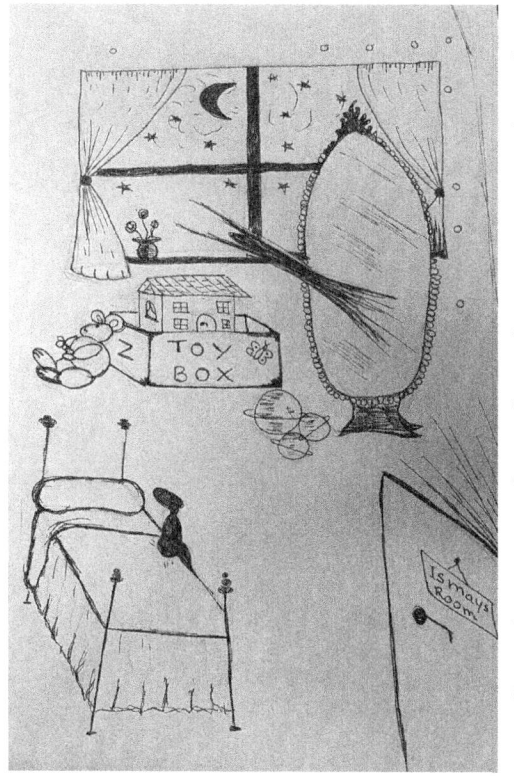

the hallway to her bedroom, washed her face, brushed her teeth and jumped straight into her bed. She was tired and knew she'd be having the most wonderful sleep. Curling into a foetal position, she closed her eyes and fell to sleep.

Morning arrived and Ismay opened her eyes. She stretched.

Wow that was such a great dream, she said as she jumped out of bed and ran down the stairs.

Passing a mirror, she took a second look and saw her five-year-old self. *I must tell Mummy and Daddy about my dream*, she said as she shouted out to her parents - they were both in the kitchen. "Mummy, Daddy, I'd the best dream ever..."

Mr Benjamin grinned, nodding his head knowingly. "Come over here and tell us all about it..."

Ismay was happy, she finally had the opportunity to talk to her parent's about her past and future life experiences...

Learning About Dyslexia: some handy information

"If you gave us the freedom to learn differently, we would not be called a person with learning difficulties but a person who learns differently"

Zoe Pennant

Dyslexia for the Wise, is a Community Interest Company (CIC) that supports children, young people and adults with Dyslexia or other learning differences. Its aim is to support and deliver through the provision of Dyslexia Diagnostic Assessments, Educational Programmes, Workshops, Art, Training and Coaching.

Their mission is to bring together academics and creativity, enabling creative thinkers known as dyslexics to flourish academically. As, even today, a lot of people still ask the question, *how do we identify the signs of dyslexia in our children or adults?*

The signs vary but can commonly include:

- Skipping words or lines;

- Reading slowly or not wanting to read at all;

- Difficulties absorbing information when needing to write it down;

- Blurring and doubling of letters or words;

- Missing out letters or words when writing;

- Letters reversing;

- Seeing different words when reading.

It can also affect memory, organisation, remembering left from right, taking instructions and giving directions. Dyslexia can also be connected to the other parts of the Dyslexia family:

- **Dyscalculia** (difficulties with Math's, telling the time and numbers);

- **Dyspraxia** (coordination and movement);

- **Dysgraphia** (inability to write coherently).

An Optometry Assessment can highlight the problems with vision but cannot diagnose Dyslexia in itself. It can detect visual problems that contribute to reading difficulties including Dyslexia, especially if the traits are missing out words, words moving on the page, having headaches or finding it easier to read large print instead of small. To get this assessment completed, one first needs to see a qualified Optometrist.

For Parents, Carers and Children

5 Things to eat and do to help children with dyslexia:

(1)   EAT HEALTHY

Walnuts

Broccoli

Avocado

Blueberries

Spinach

Tomatoes

These foods are very good for the brain.

(2)   EXERCISES

Exercises and sports are very good to energize the brain

Example:

Place right hand to your left knee

and left hand to your right knee, one after the other,

By using the left and right side of the body, this rebalances the brain.

(3) TAKE YOUR TIME

Take your time with doing school work, tidying up, working on something, anything that needs your brain to remember, allow your thinking to catch up with the brain. Patience is key, this way errors will happen less.

(4) WATER

Drink a lot of water, this helps with dehydration and gives energy to both sides of the brain.

(5) PRACTISE, PRACTISE, PRACTISE

Practise on things you are doing, this will help with the memory process. PRACTISE MAKES PERFECT!

Relevant Organisation to Contact:

Dyslexia for the Wise

Website: www.dyslexiaforthewise.org

Email: info@dyslexiaforthewise.org

Printed in Great Britain
by Amazon